821.

D0434057

FIRST THE FEATHERS

Amanda Bell

Doire Press

First published in 2017

Doire Press
Aille, Inverin
Co. Galway
www.doirepress.com

Layout & design: Lisa Frank
Cover photo: Niall Murphy
Author photo: Patrick Redmond

Printed by Clódóirí CL
Casla, Co. na Gaillimhe

ISBN 978-1-907682-56-8

CONTENTS

Dedicated to the memory of the other AB, constant companion.

Striking Out

Swimming out feels transgressive. It departs at a tangent from the edicts to stay within your depth, swim parallel to the shore, only swim on an incoming tide. It defies the ingrained need to touch down every now and then to test the depth. Once you're out of your depth, depth ceases to matter. You are a cork bobbing on the surface. You can't stop. You are literally swimming for your life, vulnerable to switching currents, rogue waves, trailing jellyfish, sudden cramps, reckless jet-skiers, effluent, seals which — in the water — loom colossal.

> sudden swirl —
> what brushes my fingers
> in dark water?

From the shore, the yellow buoys look small, and gay as bunting. Up close, they are large, grimy, and industrial. The ropes which anchor them to the seabed are slimy and barnacled. They do not invite touch.

> black cormorants
> drying on the rocks
> their bright white guano

And what of those who choose to carry on? Not the channel swimmers, coated in grease and accompanied by support craft, but those who keep on going until their last breath leaves and they transmute into flotsam. How does it go? Can you choose to breathe the sea? Or just keep swimming till the numbness spreads from each extremity up long bones to hips and shoulders, paralysing you, till finally your lungs, too, cease to function. There's no-one on the shoreline shouting stop; it's too late to change your mind.

> a passing ferry —
> behind a swell
> the horizon disappears

Points
(after Kathleen Jamie)

My arrowheads, no harsh tongues these
but tiny points for felling forest birds —
folsom and clovis, in creamy stone,
black flint and splintered chert
bound to a shaft by hide.

Arrayed before me here by hue and heft
as I renovate a printer's tray —
drawing a blade along each joint,
fine-brushing every nook and crack,
spirit swabbing to ensure a grip
for backing papers chosen to offset
the colours of each stone, cast light on
hard-struck angles.
                    Tools fallen out of use,
they take their place in ink-stained wood,
nestled in the abandoned bed of words.

First the Feathers

The woodcock lies still,
head lolling towards the weight of his long beak,
matt black eyes camouflaged in mottled brown.

I tug the silken down
against the grain with steady thumbs,
mindful not to break the cobwebbed skin.

Bared, the breasts are cool and smooth.
I crop the twiggy legs:
small claws gesture from the feather pile.

The wings I open like a book:
press down, stretch out the elegant pins,
scissor through the shoulder joint —
use a knife for the sinews and skin.

Turned over, the back is quick to pluck.
Incongruously large, the head and feathered neck —
I cut them off, the long beak faced away.

The white-mounded rump is stubbled
by pale thick-rooted quill stumps:
with the knife point I enlarge the vent,
finger out the looped beige guts.

Squeezing beneath the wings I probe
for organs, anxious
not to squash the little bundle out of shape.
How clean it seems, trussed neatly —
though I can't erase the trace
of talcum-powdered belly
from my fingers.

Sourdough

Take the softest flour,
milled salt, warm water
in a crockery bowl.

Let air flow through,
without strong drafts,
no heat, nor chill.

Then wait, till wild yeasts
conjured from the ether
spore the waiting mass

to billowing froth:
this, this is perfection,
home-grown starter;

well-formed crumb
and crust that tastes
of grains and salt and me —

this alchemy.

Peat Smoke

The words were out before I could draw them back,
above on the bog that day, turf-cutting.
I saw them coming — the little one jumped from stack to stack
and it took me back to the old place.
I was thinking of Seán then, and I said
'There's nothing like a little child
to keep you warm in bed — like a *ballín* of wool.'

It hung in the air,
turf smoke over a sulky fire.

They passed the time of day before moving off:
but they'll never smell a peat fire without picturing
a *ballín* of wool,
and wondering what harm was in me.

ballín: a small ball.

Immortality

To make durable Writing on Paper,
dissolve gum-arabic in water,
and add thereto ivory black
— extremely well ground —
and write therewith.

Acids cannot discharge this writing;
and if you wish to secure it
against the steams of hot water,
the writing may be covered
with white of egg, clarified.

To revive old Writings
which are almost defaced,
boil gall nuts in wine,
then steep a sponge into the liquor,
and pass it on the lines of the old writing:
by this method the letters
— which were almost undecipherable —
will appear as fresh as if newly done.

Mulranny

This April day the storm at last falls calm
enough to see what washed up in the gale —
tide-tumbled rocks, sea-glass rubbed smooth by waves,
driftwood light as balsam, sundry flotsam.
The machair stretches out behind low dunes
where sheep sniff sea-pinks glazed with brine;
old lids and frayed green shreds of twine
blow loose across the intertidal zone.
In a hollow, sheltered from the open sea,
a swollen ewe, eyes gone, her lamb's hind
leg protruding through her skin, reminds
me that we're close to a *cillín* — where
a monolith raised high among small stones
bears a plaque to mark unconsecrated bones.

cillín: a historical burial place in Ireland for children unbaptised at the time
of death.

Moving Statues, 1985

The summer I turned seventeen we'd make
round trips to town, for videos, and chips
from Donkey Ford's; on our way home swing by
the Ballinacurra Weston shrine, to join
the crowds assembled at the railings,
keen to see if this one, like her Ballinspittle sister,
would get off her plinth, inform mere passers-by
that the time to convert Russia had arrived.

We inched our shoulders through a crowd in thrall
to stone, not asking what — if her concrete kin
in Granard had kept schtum — could move this one
to pity mortal neediness; how, if the virgin
saints of the south-west had not joined hands
around small Joanne Hayes, we should find signs
of divine compassion here, after the pub.

Airborne, the click and slide of beads, cadences
familiar from the group at our front door,
praying for my parents' votes in '83 —
returning with my date I stood and gazed
over their shoulders, the crown of each head behaloed
in the glow of the sodium light.

Tuam

Once more we are called upon
to lay our wafers on the body politic,

take them one by one,
place them on our tongues
and absorb the failings of the state,
digest the blind-eyes turned.

All this we do, in silence,
and remembrance of you.

Incubus

What's happened? It feels quite different.
All tastes have a taint.
Low background thrum.
Warm walls don't throb or torque,
now everything's gone quiet.
No strut to brace around the shape
that was coming to define us.
Far off bright lights are strobing through the deep dark.
Now stretching out feels far too easy —
nothing offers up resistance
in this self-sealed kingdom.
The core of the matter —
if I am, or am not,
a man.

Dark Days

i.m. Savita Halappanavar

Suspended at the end of Krishna Paksha,
the moon is a sickle
freeze-framed in the night sky.

The fireworks have been cancelled,
replaced by candles
and a vision of you
dancing on the cusp.

These are dark days
between Diwali and Advent,
waiting

   for the moon to wax.

Moon

I am caught off-guard sometimes,
by a shard glimpsed between trees
or behind chimneys. As dawn breaks,
or in the clear blue hue of afternoon,
she watches me. I walk into the road
at night to see her lying low, or crane
from a window in the early hours,
wondering where she's hiding now.
Elusive, she changes shape, and colour —
the pewter of a beaten lid, gold of ripened quince.
She steals into my room to touch my things,
grows larger, as I approach the horizon.
One day I shall open up the shutters —
be confronted by her pitted face.

The Ballad of Mary Anne Cadden

You'll have heard about this woman — Nurse Cadden was her name —
Regarded as a killer, spoken of with shock and shame.

But the way she's been depicted deserves some scrutiny —
There were many facets to her, as you shall shortly see.

Entrepreneuse or criminal, feminist or quack?
You can draw your own conclusions, but consider first the facts.

She was born in Pennsylvania, in eighteen ninety-one,
Then returned to County Mayo, where her family owned a farm.

They settled in Doonbredia, under Nephin Mountain,
And opened up a grocer's shop, where Mamie learned accounting.

She ran the shop near Lahardane till she was thirty-four,
But country life was not for her, she clearly wanted more.

She qualified in Holles Street a midwife for to be —
She loved the buzz of city life, and lively company.

She opened up a nursing home, attracting many clients,
Then invested in a fine big house on the main street in Rathmines.

She called the house 'Maelruin' — they came from near and far,
And with the proceeds of the job she bought herself a car:

A red MG she brought from Wales and drove with some panache —
Letting it be known that she was raking in the cash.

One day the car was recognised way out in County Meath,
Near where a baby girl was found in the gateway to a field.

Charged with child abandonment, Mamie was sent to prison —
The guards went in to search her house and dug up the back garden.

Although they found a foetus there no charge was ever brought —
'Twas only for the living child she came before the court.

Forced to sell the nursing home to pay her legal fees,
It ended any chance she had of growing old with ease.

She was sentenced to hard labour for the year she spent inside,
Then the Central Board expelled her as a registered midwife.

Forbidden now to practise but still young and energetic,
She set herself up once again, but as a paramedic.

She treated dandruff, skin disease, VD and constipation,
And it was she you went to see to get a termination.

She worked out of a basement suite on Lower Pembroke Street,
Then placed ads in the *Evening Mail*, but kept them quite discreet.

And Dublin's finest medicos sent her their referrals —
She saw widows, married women, the well-off and working girls.

But a girl with an infection was admitted to the Coombe,
And told the guards what Cadden did in her consulting rooms.

This lead to Mamie's second trial in nineteen forty-five,
The sentence that was handed down was five more years inside.

Completely on her uppers by the time she was released,
She started working once again from a bedsit on Hume Street.

It was only one year later that Brigid Breslin died,
Her corpse was found on Hume Street, no-one was ever tried —

But suspicion rose that Mamie was still practising her trade
In her hovel of a bedsit and with someone else's aid.

For a certain man was questioned about the girl who died —
His address was in her handbag, his car was seen outside.

It was he who Mamie called on when she lost another woman —
He came early the next morning to help with the removal.

The deceased — Helen O'Reilly — a mother of six chislers —
Had sought out Mamie's service but an embolism killed her.

And so in May of fifty-six another charge was brought —
Of murder, against Cadden, and she came once more to court.

The mob was out to get her though the evidence was scrappy.
They demanded retribution — only hanging'd make them happy.

Nine days of evidence was heard, from the prosecution,
The jury found her guilty — the sentence: execution.

Her lawyers mounted an appeal against a death so brutal.
After protests to the President the sentence was commuted.

A life in prison lay in store but after just one year
They transferred her to the Mental, for reasons still unclear.

Compared to Mountjoy Prison the conditions there were fine,
And she died there one year later, in nineteen fifty-nine.

No doubt another took her place, demand was always there,
And the UK was an option, for those who had the fare.

But when you talk of women's rights, and argue to and fro,
Remember that death sentence, passed just sixty years ago.

Mount Jerome

When the summer course in taxidermy
came unstuck, it seemed appropriate
to mark your fiftieth birthday
with another type of preservation:
continuing a lifelong fascination
with the dead, from fruitless excavations
in the bog to Victorian cemetery visits.
To move from Mount Jerome to Père Lachaise
to Highgate would triangulate
your half centenary, confer stability
on the increasingly shaky premise
that anything in life remains unchanged —
that we haven't reached a parting of the ways.
If I had a bag of rounded stones
I'd work them in my hand like beads —
lay them, palm warm, on top of every grave
I visit. The tap of stone on stone —
my calling card — expecting no response
though aiming to connect.
The sharp report more definite
than pots of flowers
or garlands of embellished beads:
each saint's face weathered to a death's head.

Mortuary Virgin

I thought to find you in a drawer
with a tag on your toe,
but no.

There was a candle and a cross,
an imitation chapel,
a silk-lined box.

I touched your statue hands —
in my mind's eye, they clutch a handbag.
Your eyes are closed —
taking a moment out before your lift arrives.

Seedlings

The woman at the door explains that she was once a lodger in what is now our dining-room. She asks to see the room, where she gave birth to her daughter almost thirty years ago. My second daughter was born in that same room, the shutterless windows of which look out over the back garden; later that winter we dug a hole and placed her placenta, unfurled in its glorious purple strangeness, among the balled-roots of an ornamental cherry tree against the back wall of the house. Her older sister, whose placenta had been left behind in hospital, was put out by this, so she too had a tree planted in her honour: a morello, which grew to fruit prolifically.

> a flash of scarlet
> in the blackbird's open bill —
> cherry season

The garden, like the house, is Victorian, planted with fruit trees and rhubarb stools, and surrounded by rubble-granite walls in which valerian has self-seeded. At night snails surge out from the old stone and overrun the garden, feasting on our seedlings and tender plants. Late one autumn a friend gifts us a young hedgehog, thinking it will eat the snails. The creature is doomed by her lack of fat reserves, and some weeks later a tiny foot is noticed protruding from a pile of leaves — not hibernating, but dead. We dig a small hole beneath the morello cherry tree, and bury her there.

> from the bonfire
> white ash blown
> All Soul's Day

When we first came here the flowerbeds were riddled with tiny fragments of glass, remnants of a greenhouse demolished so long ago that the pieces were quite blunt. It took years of sifting and enriching to restore the soil quality.

> tumbling from my spade
> a burnished centipede
> this winter digging

The greenhouse was a relic of the previous occupants, a farming family from Cork. The man of the house had an association with Nurse Cadden. At the time of the first criminal investigation into her activities, the back garden of her Rathmines premises was excavated, and a foetus unearthed. It was a girl.

spinning from the tree
sycamore keys
thunder brewing

The Darkness

In winter I awaken to the dread
of losing something indefinable,
and darkness stretches out around my bed.

September flips a trip switch in my head
and daily living seems less feasible;
in winter I awaken to the dread.

On All Souls' Night I'd gladly hide instead
of letting on that I'm invincible,
as darkness stretches out around my bed.

By December, it's as if the world were dead:
to fight the darkness seems unthinkable.
Each winter day I struggle with the dread.

I wish that I could hibernate instead
of coming to and feeling vulnerable
to darkness stretching out around my bed.

I try to think of shorter nights ahead
though springtime now seems inconceivable.
In winter I awaken to the dread
of darkness stretching out around my bed.

A Ghazal of Exodus

Cradled in a rush ark, in the leaf-green Nile, Moses
floats downstream, where parted reeds disclose him near to home.

*

A Chalayan[1] coffee-table can be donned and worn —
saving time when on short notice to leave home.

*

In nineteen forty-seven *SS Exodus* sets
sail for Palestine, the closest it can get to home.

*

Leaving Babylon behind, the Rastafarians
turn their eyes to Ethiopia, their Zion home.

*

Shark-shoals follow coffin-ships, feeding on the bodies
of the dead, thrown overboard en route from home.

*

Bibles open at *Exodus*, St Kildans
bid farewell to their remote Atlantic island home.

*

Millions of the displaced become convinced
that an over-laden boat is safer than their home.

*

Silence in Calais jungle, where stitched-up lips protest
at bull-dozed shanties — the makeshift substitute for home.

*

Do we not hear alarm bells when this Earth's people surge
across the globe, flowing like the rain away from home?

[1] Hussein Chalayan is the maker of a set of portable furniture, inspired by the
designer's thinking on the wartime impermanence that finds homes raided and
families forced to flee or be killed.

Dreaming

(after Hokusai's *Dream of the Fisherman's Wife*)

Grinding the octopus against a rock
to tenderize its dense white flesh, he sees
the clustered suckers on its arms, and baulks
to contemplate the breadth of what it feels.
Onshore she dreams him diving deep for pearls,
lungs closed, eyes wide, hands combing through the weed
where oysters are concealed, their ridged shells curled
around each tiny iridescent seed.
The artist halts with blade in hand, to think
how images cut into wood with steel
will come to life where paper meets the inked
woodblock — his inner reveries revealed.
The dreamless sea embraces every grain
of sand — more salt than blood, wetter than rain.

Troglodytes

(On visiting Lascaux cave for the 70th anniversary of its discovery)

Inland, the road torcs into forest.
Among walnut trees, the house vibrates
with life: bees, hummingbird moths,
an infestation of squat black crickets.
They love the shade of cool clay tiles
and watch us sleep, eat, bathe, make love.
We sweep them out at night — they won't jump,
just scuttle, and keep returning.

Deep in the lamplit chamber, shadows
in the knotted scaffolding, they watched
hands palpate the limestone for flanks, spines,
manes — and draw them into life.

And when the lamps guttered, they scurried
over aurochs, bison, the inverted horse,
till a dog arrived, with boys and lights,
and they were brushed aside —
not far, but out of sight,
waiting for night to fall.

Winter Citrus

I keep a brazier in every room
to warm me through the winter.
Citrus — glowing in baskets, bowls,
on plates, in shades of flame.

Marmalade oranges with foamy rind,
the raw-silk of Sanguinello
shot through with crimson,
the dull sheen of clementines,
point-nosed Sicilian lemons,
southern hues imbued with sun.

Blended with northern stores
— of almonds, sugar, flour —
to cakes, and curds and marmalades,
they ward off breakdown, frozen
on the year's hard shoulder.

Solstice

Tonight there is no compass —
stars camouflaged by satellites, late planes.

Beams follow foxes on night trails,
surveillance helicopters light up lanes.

In tinselled houses, on the brink
of life, machines — on standby — hum.

Awakened by the glow, I lose
my bearings to deceitful twilight

and long to sink in blackness,
in deepest dark to feel, before I see,

stealing along a stone-lined passage:
the inkling of a creeping shaft of spring.

Winter Sun

At winter's end I dreamed I loved you —
spring tense, leaning in
to sense your musk,
the dry heat you radiate.

By dream logic you were called away
but held me first —
you'd thought it would be otherwise.
Desolate, I awoke, and found myself

within your arms — a relief so vast
that twenty years flashed past my eyes
in all the tiny gestures
that pass mostly unremarked,

as you opened up the shutters,
watched early sun break through the mist.

Sindhura, Andalusia

I think I know now what it is I love
about this place — not just the play of light
reflected from the fractured sea with shadow
from the corded hills, where eagles cast
their silhouettes on sunflower fields, intent
on hunting though the sun beats down.

Sated swallows, ready for the short flight down
to Africa, make practice sallies that you love
to watch, while cattle-egrets stalk, intently
grubbing dung for bugs and ticks — alighting
on the ridged spines of their hosts till, cast
off with a twitch, they flutter to the shade.

The first time that we came here, overshadowed
by a PET scan, although we were dragged down
by fear, the prospect of a respite cast
an easy grace about us both, my love,
holding us static in a cone of light
where every breath was achingly intense.

Released into senescence, and intent
on following the sun to brink of shade,
absorbing every fragile point of light,
each summer we continue to return, down
to Sindhura, not overthinking why we love
this forge in which our lives were cast.

But when the airborne sand of the Levante casts
its pall around us all, as if intent
on blinding us to everything we love
to see, I know this is a transient shade,
that the windstorm will eventually die down
and landmarks re-emerge into clear light.

Now I love to gaze out from the cooling shade,
intently watching as the sun slides down,
while soft moths cast themselves towards the light.

The Austringer

(In 1937 T.H. White set out to break a goshawk, using the long-superseded meth.
of depriving the bird of sleep.)

White knew it could take several days
to break the goshawk, whose dandelion eye
flared in the barn's dim light
as he bated stubbornly
with all his feathered weight,
so neither bird nor man could rest.

Stealth alone could lull him down to rest —
a contest that went on for days.
White's only weapon was to wait,
show no impatience, keep an eye
on how the goshawk stubbornly
rejected the temptation to alight.

Cloistered in a barn with little light,
by the second day White yearned for rest
but like the hawk persisted, stubbornly,
somnambulant through nights and days,
watching his challenger with heavy eye —
his only strategy: to wait.

To bring the bird down he must wait
till it was willing to alight.
So neither met the other's eye —
hubris struggling with desire to rest.
The will to power went on for days,
both man and bird resisting stubbornly,

until, without surrender, stubbornly
the goshawk sank his flagging weight
on outstretched arm. Through sleep-shot daze
the austringer could see the light —
the prospect of elusive rest
for bone-tired limb and blood-rimmed eye.

Likewise in the early hours, I,
too, am wrestling stubbornly
with sleep, but find no rest.
Goshawk or austringer? I wait
to see who will yield first, but soon it's light —
grey scaling between nights and days.

On whose whim do the sleepless wait
so stubbornly to rest, impervious to dark and light?
What yellow eye seen through a daze?

The sleepless

watch cats stalking walls,
lean back to feel the needling burst
of let-down milk, the starfish hand
on marbled breast,
and cup the downy head;

wait, till the book's heft
drags on weary wrists
then lay it down, and
start the nightly shift
from room to room;

cross shoe-strewn landings,
still the dripping taps,
explore dim corners
as streetlights slide through
ill-met shutters;

descend the darkly
unfamiliar stairs, stroke piano keys
but fail to find a tune;
while outside, passing taxis
cause the walls to light and dim,

like the sleepers,
breathing out, breathing in.

The beauty of the game

is lost on me when I watch you play:
I see the curve of your cheek,
the rounded base of your skull
— once a custom-fit for my palm —
and feel again the warm weight of your incipience.

No more walnut-snug in my armour
your head now bobs around the pitch,
the air shrieks with the thwack of
plastic against wood,
against bone.

Cochlea

Silent at the tunnel's end,
long-stilled filaments stir —
the current wafts them into life and ripples on.
Outside, kinetic leaves begin to creak
like a kindler's twisted sticks
just failing to combust,
frail branches groan with the weight of wrens.
Wind-caught hair tears against my head,
and strafing seagulls screech above it.

Into this strife, like a diver I emerge
from pounding blood and roaring quiet,
and now I dread it,
                    the din of dinner time,
the chaos of preparation.
Plates detonate on tables,
spotlights penetrate
my skull's thin skin.
Pulled roughly, cutlery explodes,
glinting metal shards erupt,
a heavy handle hits the floor —
its slo-mo bounce
vibrates my vertebrae
like cymbals.
Teeth grind like large hard nails on chalk boards,
the slop of saliva,
artillery fire of glasses missing coasters,
the sickening slide of drops
from rim to base.
All is glass and metal,
and my fingers grope for plastic —
dialling for a setting
to tune out.

New Road

like this new road. Unlike the old
it can't recall the frozen fields
where children skate in treadless boots.

This pavement has no sheltered gates
where teens, entwined like sap-filled weeds
explore warm flesh beneath their coats.

I love this overpass because from here
I cannot see the house where once we were
and thought we'd always be.

I like the roaring ring-road:
it drowns out the echoes of our lives,
disperses them like smoke.

I'm glad this road just carries on,
oblivious to abandoned dreams,
and cannot haunt what it once knew.

I love its lack of looking back. How
it cuts so cleanly through the ties
that connect me, still, to you.

Mulcair

Teens of the 1980s swam in jeans —
our Riviera was the weir at Ballyclough,
where we clambered weedy rocks and dove from trees,
sloped off to smoke and throw sticks into the millstream:
each day at four the river water ran from brown to red.

The salmon steps were our jacuzzi, where a slender boy
was held under by the current, re-emerging blue
and slower. His life moved one beat down to the factory:
Ballyclough Meats — leaning over walls
we watched him sluicing down the concrete:
each day at four the river water ran from brown to red.

In pools beyond the stone bridge lampreys clung to the submerged rocks:
we dislodged them with rod butts
                              till they coiled round our wellies,
tumbled them onto the lawn at home.

In our houses we sloughed off our damp silty clothing. Forgetful
of our monstrous quarry, dying slowly on the grass.
Each day at four the river water ran from brown to red.

Starting Secondary School

That would have been the summer that we piled into the trailer
parked beside the combine harvester — let showers of grain
cascade over our heads, a *pot pourri* of wheat and earwigs,
beetles, dust and mice, and it was paradise.

Jack's fall from the barn was the first blow to our cavorting —
both collarbones was all he broke but when Bill slipped from the horsebox
something worse cracked on the road.

                                August came hard after July:
they felled the tree where John's da hanged, though the overpass soon took its
place.
Milch cows flicked their shit-encrusted tails, worm-shot mushrooms blackened
in rank grass,
pigs shrieked, the ponies bucked and bit, and rabbits stripped the cabbage field,
while ticks embedded in our sweaty flesh, leaving welts beneath the wool
of new school uniforms — expensive gabardines we'd never wear.
As elderberries purpled, phone-lines sagged with strings of swallows
getting ready to migrate, and go they did.

Pointillisme

Rouen, 1989. The cobbles have yet to be disturbed by metro works. Mauve fog folds into the city basin and drapes over the points of the Gothic cathedral. As I descend to the *centre ville* through the *Jardin des Plantes*, Pan's bust leers through the mist.

> through the half light —
> magnolia petals
> shivering

We crush into a booth lit by red paper lanterns, and devour platters of food — sour, bitter, sweet, salty, spicy. Our mouths shine bright with grease. Afterwards, espresso. As the cup is drained of its hot black liquor, shunga appear.

> restaurant fish tank —
> the rasping tongues of molluscs
> on the glass

ntom

I think of you as I undress, or showering,
as my soapy palms sweep foam from pit to pit:
I watch fat droplets glide along each breast
then trickle down my front and out of sight.
Like you, I've felt the tightening grip of ice-cold sea
firm up my flesh; known the heat of lovers' fingertips
and lips; observed the loosening, milk-wet mouths
of infants drowsing from my nipple into sleep.

Core-deep memories. Where do they go to,
when the flesh where they took root has been excised?
If an amputated limb continues itching,
and a missing breast still tenses in the chill,
I fear that what survives of us may not, in fact,
be love, but a disembodied longing to be held.

Canicule
(Lot et Garonne, 2003)

Hot mercury oozed in glossy beads
from a cracked tube on our terrace
by a pool which slowly bloomed
to algal green. At dawn, after a storm,
I swam laps, then — coming up for breath —
resurfaced by a snake washed off the hill.
While some succumbed to heatstroke
we remained indoors, took showers,
ate well-chilled melon in the shade;
watched, through slatted shutters,
ripe figs flop from off the tree, and bake
in honeyed union with parched grass, till
borne away as sugar crumbs, by ants
who knew such days would never last.

Canicule: French for heatwave

Still trailing drains, fresh out of ICU,
my father asks 'What age is he? Yer man
in the O2?' He's seventy-nine, Dad,
just like you. 'And is his voice as good
as in his prime?' Yes, I say, and it's true:
it's a gravelled river flowing past
the milestones of inexpertly rolled joints,
tentative afternoon deflowerings.

Now losses are less sweet and firsts endured:
the first fall, first distressed phone-call.
So tonight the offspring of the agèd
close their eyes against the old man's mask onstage,
and from their tiers in the O2 set forth
upstream against the current of themselves.

So Long

The first gannet was a juvenile. It was sitting on wet sand below Lissadell House, quite alone. Its wings and back were dappled with dark brown, its breast and head dazzling white. A black line extended from the root of its long grey beak to encircle each ice-blue eye. I drew close to see whether it might be injured. It extended both wings to their full span, raised itself on long striped toes, and lunged at me, before resettling in its damp hollow.

I rejoined the crowd, took my place in the tiered seating, and waited for the concert, but when I think back on that night it isn't of Leonard Cohen in profile against the backdrop of Ben Bulben, or the drunk woman screaming for 'Marianne', or even the tailback of traffic leaving Sligo in the rain, headlights forming a giant glowing caterpillar which squirmed into the distance of the Ox Mountains, but the image of that blue-grey beak, strong enough to pierce the sea at sixty miles an hour.

> barely a ripple —
> turning frosted seaglass
> in my palm

The second gannet was an adult. I came across it as I walked the high tide mark at Mulranny. Previous excursions had yielded bleached driftwood, a dead pilot whale, small cetacean bones, a cow's skull, and a perfect skeletal sea urchin. And this time, a dead gannet, its yellowed head just visible beneath a heavy dusting of sand. Its powerful neck, sinuous, seemed more furry than feathered, reminding me that the St Kildans used gannet necks as footwear. Having neither pocket knife nor bag with me, I turned it over with my foot, admired its impenetrably dense feathers, its folded black feet, and walked on. But halfway back to the car desire won out. I doubled back, deciding to drag the bird back to the car by the very beak that I so coveted, and then figure out how to get it home.

It was very heavy. I tried to convince myself that the stench was of rotten seaweed, or the wind from an overladen septic tank, but soon had to admit that the bird, for all that it was intact, reeked of decay. Undeterred, I shifted it from hand to hand to share the weight between my shoulders, but just as the carpark appeared ahead, with a sickening slide the heavy rotting creature slipped its skull bone out of the keratinous sheath of the beak, and slumped to the ground, leaving me holding a pale scabbard, the weight and texture of a fingernail.

I brought the frail beak-form home and buried it in a flowerpot until the stench evaporated. When I dug it up, it had faded and frayed like a wind-torn plastic bag. Nevertheless, it has taken its place on the mantelpiece between a gull's skull and some whale vertebrae, and is curiously beautiful, though I still can't detach the sight of it from the feel of that heavy body sliding away.

by the light
of guttering embers
bones cast shadows

Cockle Picking

Look first for an open cockle shell
spreadeagled on the damp part of the strand,
then, with your fingers, form a claw,
to dredge the soupy layers of the sand:
below the meniscus, bunched like fists,
their little clumps feel weighty in the palm.

It rained when I brought you cockling —
how fast the mist erased you from my sight —
then you happened on the picture-postcard
seaweed man, who stopped his ass-cart,
asked you for a light.
You leaned in, not expecting
him to seize you, or the strength
with which he held you, like a vice.

I think of you whenever I go cockling,
soft and shivering in your crackling plastic mack —
you thought he'd hide you under piles of gleaming seakelp,
while he waited for the cold tide to flow back.

...asion

Everything we thought we knew about the Vikings was wrong... it is simply not the case that there wasn't a Viking presence in Ireland outside Dublin, Waterford, Wexford and Limerick. Vikings settled the west coast and integrated with the native Irish.'   — *The Irish Times*

What I'd like to know about the Vikings
is what happened to their furs,
because yours aren't faring well.

When, after all these years,
I reach back through the wardrobe
to run my fingers through the deep,
soft pile, slip them inside
velvet pockets, feel myself
once more with bowed head
lower than the beeswaxed pew,
leaning in to breathe an echo of *Rive Gauche* —

instead my nails get snagged on grit.
Inspecting them by summer light
I see that moths have burrowed in
and infiltrated every seam,
denuding patches in their wake.

Ploughing both hands through the pelt,
disturbing waves of frass,
I pluck at roots of silk cocoons,
then, catching them by small black dots,
pull naked maggots from their pods.

As I unpick each seam the frail skin rips,
and though I light no funeral pyre,
I'm cupping dust.

The Spalted Man

Resin studs in the cherry's bronze skin,
gold rings in purple ribbons.
The thud and crack of the swinging axe,
winter wood needs splitting.

The moss-furred crust of the ancient thorn,
its splayed white curds a-gleaming.
The thud and crack of the swinging axe,
winter wood needs splitting.

The spalted beech, felled by winds last spring
is filigreed, etched and rotten.
The thud and crack of the swinging axe,
winter wood needs splitting.

Beyond the mountain lives a man
whose winter wood needs splitting,
and I am a crumb at his hollow core —
forgotten, though he's living.
The thud and crack of the swinging axe,
winter wood needs splitting.

...ery, the Importance of

Men were supposed to wield long knives,
preside at table, carve thin slices sidelong.
Yet when my father handed on the role
I didn't yield my brother space, and with
a small sharp kitchen knife excised
the white meat from the bone
in one long piece, and on a board
I carved the breast from right to left:
each portion of an equal size,
each with its strip of crisp bronze skin.
I removed the legs, deboned
the thighs, and piled a platter high
with white meat, brown meat, drummers,
wings, and chunks of stuffing packed with nuts.
My task was executed well.
Why, then, the small sharp twist of shame
that I cut the flesh against the grain?

A Small Attendance

i.m. Kingsley Scott

There is a vacancy for an old man in my life:
I hadn't realised until today when books arrived
by morning post, sent from a recent friend.

They will join the set of *Littérature Française*
passed on when you moved to a first-floor flat,
chosen for the view, not emphysema.

To have a companion so much my senior
seems normal now, even familial —
as heads tilt in for quiet conversations,

more ordinary than those dinners you prepared
when I was seventeen: sherry and *ras al hanout-*
tempered stews, Moustaki on the stereo.

My father waited anxiously —
cheroot-tip glowing as I hiccupped my way in —
when you dropped me home in the tiny car

you folded into like *Monsieur Hulot*,
draped in the dark red jumper which you wore
from my first year in school until retirement.

I think you were wearing it in Marrakech
when I came down by train in '89,
with the blissful abandon of a run-away.

We bussed to Agadir to escape the Easter cold,
ate preserved lemons in a pungent tagine,
bitter and more salt than I could bear.

The last time I went to see you there, I brought
your meds from home. You had travelled alone
with your oxygen tank, I had a family in tow.

You chose not to say goodbye to me when you returned
to die — your obituary side-swiped me over breakfast.
Like so many stories, yours ends in Mount Jerome:
the Brandenburg concertos, a small attendance.

Hero

The sailor on the box of Navy Cut
peered from my grandfather's top pocket,
our lookout on the bog road.

One hand in his, in the other bog cotton,
white bearded heads dancing in the wind,
as I sprang from hummock to hummock,

unaware of brackish water just below.
When I lost a boot to the sucking bog
he swept me up to shoulder-ride me home.

At night, I'd watch him dozing —
hand resting on the chair arm, as
grey ash curled to a worm cast.

I watched the pulse tick at his temple,
heard the whistle of his breathing,
wished this breezy day might never end.

ountain Sheep

The holiday rental in Dingle was just above the cloud-line, where the drizzling grey days of summer were indistinguishable one from the other. Still an only child, each morning I had to travel the length of a glazed corridor to rouse the grown-ups. Afraid to look out over the misty fields, I ran all the way, feet slapping in the silence.

the scarecrow's ravaged face   what has he seen?

Pipistrelles

Night is the shadow of the earth
and winter just a tilt against the sun —
although the soul curls inwards on itself
it's nothing personal. As pipistrelles

vacate their common roosts
once dark of night extends its reach —
and seek, instead, forsaken nooks
where they cling, like leaves, undead.

Bumblebees

There was no need to fret about the bees —
their fragile nest, unlidded
as I pulled weeds beneath the apple tree,
their squirming larvae naked
to my gaze and to the sun.

They watched me from the border
while I hastily replaced the roof,
before returning to rethread
the fibres of their grassy home.

In the cleared weeds I see
their entrance and their exit,
how their flight paths sweep
the garden in an arc, stitching up
the canvas of this space, as if
they could remake the world
which lies in shreds around us.

The dome moves, as I watch it,
the stretching of an inchoate form —
when morning comes
it glistens with white dew.

Buttercups

Buttercups spread overground as well as under —
runners take long leaps, bite down for purchase, leap again,
white clustered roots form galaxies below.

Fork-loosened soil admits my fingers —
I work them underneath and gently tug, then throw,
over my shoulder a mountain quickly grows,
of tangled green trajectories, tufted white nebulae.

The cleared soil is friable, beetle-riddled, rich —
there will again be beans, pebble-smooth potatoes,
stubborn beetroot, white-spined chard in rows.

The buttercups throw long green ropes,
dig-in winter camps.
In spring, their golden satellites
will signal to the sky.

The moon draws tides across the shifting globe —
seeds burst, seas die,
I'm throwing weeds over my shoulder,
they regroup just out of sight.

Hidden

The derelict building used to be a nursing home, deep in the recesses of which, among the maze of corridors and bedrooms, a small synagogue nestled. Sold during the property boom, years pass before a new development begins on the site of the Victorian edifice.

low sun beams
puncturing the retained façade
blue squares

This winter solstice, I notice that a fig tree in the garden of the former home, crushed and cut back in the course of construction works, is spiked with six-inch shoots. When the demolition began, neighbours sought unsuccessfully to have a preservation order issued for the tree. I have enjoyed walking beneath it in all seasons, and am pleased by its recovery. It is a Brown Turkey fig, whose fruits announce themselves early in the year as hard green knots, appearing on bare branches at the same time as new leaves. By the time the leaves have unfurled, their protective canopy conceals the ripening fruit from both birds and passers-by, until they turn dark purple-brown, and fall onto the pavement, followed later in the season by the foliage.

underfoot
crisp leaves return to dust
warm scent rising

Last summer, with tacit permission to harvest the figs, my daughter climbed onto the wall and disappeared into the canopy in search of fruit while I waited below, basket in hand, struck by how completely she vanished. The fig leaf as a metaphor for concealment is pervasive, and the fruit itself, with its slightly venous velvet exterior, and complex interior structure, has long been used to symbolise both male and female sex organs.

afternoon sun
silken-skinned fruit
warm to the touch

Though we think of the fig as a fruit, it is an inflorescence — a bulbous stem encapsulating a cluster of flowers and seeds — and requires a particular form of pollination. Each species of fig has its own wasp; the queen enters through a tiny otiole in the base of the fruit, lays eggs and deposits pollen. Work complete, she dies and is absorbed into the fig's flesh. Fossil evidence suggests this relationship between fig and wasp has changed little in thirty-four million years.

pollen sacs
through orange amber
still, visible

Why *Ajo Blanco?*

Because of budbreak,
pushing dried husks off the branches,
first pale blossoms opening
around the fluff of yellow stamens,
blue-tits plucking out the fibres —
a downed green hull, cleft like a chin,
soft as a piglet, pinkly splitting
for the clean, brown nut revealed
beneath the crisp crisp green, the white parts.
Because of pale pink sheaths of garlic —
creamy flesh, green inner spike
of next year's bulb sprung from this clove —
feathered stems of garlic drying,
feel of long shoots sere and strawlike,
how it bends, how pliant woven,
each head nestling with the others
as I bind it into tresses.
Because of salty crystals gleaming —
white salt, pale pink almond blossoms —
paper fibre, grey-shot, flossy,
flying fluff of dandelions — sandy picnics,
salt we scraped from drying rock-pools,
saffron streaks of purple urchins,
shrimps which turn from clear to pink
to perfect shore-food wrapped
up in a screw of parchment —
parchment fine as sheaths
around the cloves of
garlic, almond petals,
glaze of seasalt —
because of budbreak.

Ajo Blanco: a Spanish no-cook soup made with almonds, raw garlic and salt.

Cuckoo

On bake days
　　pastry trimmings,
　　　salty sweet,
　　　melted beneath
　　　your pink tongue
　　as you watched her
　peeling Bramleys,
gullet raised to catch
the coils of bright green skin.
　All she touched
　　was toothsome,
　　　down to cut-off
　　　　sandwich crusts
　　　　you gathered up
　　　for bird food,
　　sucking chewy wedges
　as you ran.
Outside, while robins
　sparred for ground,
　a cuckoo chick,
　　huge in its nest,
　　　screeched anguish
　　　at the hapless dam
　　no longer fit
　　to sate its growing
needs — a meadow pipit,
egg-tooth cowed,
now baffled by
　the vector of
　　her fledgeling's
　　　maiden flight.

Changed

The world changed while I watched it —
huge and patterned above my tilted face
as she clambered from the bath.

The taut-skinned globe peaked sharply —
like the arched neck of the rocking horse
who shared my bed that winter:
the only one of them who I could trust.

Otto Weidt's Workshop for the Blind

I. Grooming Brush
The polished wooden handle fits your palm,
its woven strap lies close against your knuckles,
recalling how you'd smooth the glossy withers,
hot breath from shivering muzzle on your neck.

II. Shaving Brush
Rounding the bristle clump the hairs feel warm,
like a cat's tail drawn through your fingers,
or the silken ear of a dog, his head in your lap —
before the order to give up pets was passed.

III. Floor Brush
The broom-handle that you bind with twine feels strong,
makes you feel safe, and yet they're always on your trail.
And though the bell is rung when the Gestapo call,
it only gives you time to hide if you can hear.

IV. Close Brush
Otto argues that he needs you for the war effort,
fobs them off with banter and backhanders
while you pack into the space behind the workshop,
barely breathing as the walls close in around you.

*(During the Second World War in Berlin the brushmaker Otto Weidt employed
mainly blind and deaf Jews. As danger grew, Weidt looked for hiding places for
his employees, including a secret room at the end of his workshop.)*

Complicit

When my stolen gun
was unearthed,
tarp-wrapped,

my hands recalled
the satin of its patinated
stock, the greasy feel

of the canvas bag
I used to carry shells;
soft drift of down

from felled wild fowl,
which rolled up into rags
at my cold touch.

I wonder, in the weft of prints,
what links my hands
to shallow graves —

but this is titillating guilt,
which doesn't implicate
my green-washed life

in drowned Pacific islands,
with each switch I flick,
each spark of my ignition.

Before the Storm

Beasts look up, winds shift, dark shadows stain
the surface of the sea. Waves tilt like plates,
the water is as hard as board and heavy
as a wall of reeling vertigo; cold bodies slide
the sharp incline of shifting planks.

It's coming, twisting, flinging us aside —
detritus of humanity, small splintered dreams
wrenched free of gravity's restraint,
cast off in blackened tatters
with the smuts from Moloch's fire.

Polytunnel

Hunkered in black sludge,
I excavate a walkway,
unearth the old path.

Hand to bristled root,
I draw out thistles till
the air is thick with down.

Algae-green plastic
responds to my soft brushing,
allows light in through

bays stained by tufted
reed heads, ghost paws, powdered
wings of batting moths.

Gold fennel pollen
anoints me. Beatified,
I bear out felled wands.

Burren Vulture

Captive at the raptor centre,
far from the *dakhma,*
you hop among spectators —
plucked neck undulating towards
your prehistoric head.

The crowd gasps at your wingspan,
as you wheel among their infants —
heedless of their softness,
their downy fontanelles.

Far from the *dakhma,*
do the stacked bones of Poulnabrone
stir ancestral echoes
of sun-scorched carrion,
clean-picked skulls?

Captive at the raptor centre,
your bone-splintering bill
is a thrill for the punters;
back home the skies are empty,
and wild dogs are on the rise.

dakhma: also called a Tower of Silence, a raised, circular structure built by
Zoroastrians for dead bodies to be exposed to carrion birds.

Nefertiti's Lapdogs

So many of us share our beds with animals —
enjoy their fur against our skin, witness
their gentle dream squeals, rising odours,
and disregard their drool-soaked toys,
the litterdust still clinging to their paws.
For you it was your poodles – now lined up
in little boxes, waiting to join you
in your last repose, like Nefertiti's lapdogs,
resin-coated by her side.
And as their caskets crumble — their long-cold
ashes sink into your dust — you'll be
walking them across the sky,
that arthritic shoulder back in line,
their leads bespangled like the Milky Way.

Albus Bell *d. 21 March 2017*

Forty-nine, and tilting towards a life
defined by absences: not least of you,
small friend, with whom I've spent
more time than any other living thing.
In these last few weeks you lost a tooth,
and then a weakness in the legs became
pronounced, requiring help to stand
or drink a little broth. On Tuesday last
you died here in the bed from which I write
and look out on your grave —
a sun-warmed spot I thought you'd like,
curled up inside a wicker basket lined
with fur and silk because so intimate a friend
should have such things, for comfort,
and a little sprig of garden flowers to match
your lilac coat – anemones, fritillaries, white
cyclamen, small buds that bloomed
the day you died: the solstice, and my birthday.

Crow

Twelve months after the last shedding
I inscribe you in my skin, hooded one,
who from the shading canopy observe
your fledgeling young try out their wings.
Your monochrome disguise deters
close scrutiny — the brash pink jay your foil,
while you, unseen, craft tools for winkling
grubs, calculate the drop
required to crack a nut.
Black ink faded to slate grey refreshed
through further needling, skeletal
shades of white etched through dull matt
outline each feather's vane. It stings.
Scoring you into my breastbone,
down each hard knot on my spine,
a wing to run from scapula to coccyx, poised,
and ready.

Through the Looking Glass

The outcome would be different now — the dog destroyed,
after she burst clear through the glazed porch-door
in her haste to see who'd rung the bell, piercing
the child who stood there with a shower of sharp projectiles,
though she herself escaped almost unscathed.

Unlike my father who, when his turn came
to run through glass, ruined a brand new work suit
but continued to the counter, placed his order
for a burger, leaving in his wake a stardust trail
of diamonds bathed in ruby blood.

But other breakthroughs, bloodless, leave no clues,
more like pushing through clear membranes
till they stretch to breaking point, let you pass
straight through — not scarred, unwitnessed,
just less visible, for all that you're more you.

ACKNOWLEDGEMENTS

Acknowledgements are due to the editors of the following publications in which some of these poems, or versions thereof, appeared: *Banshee, Blithe Spirit, The Burning Bush 2, The Clearing, The Curlew, Contemporary Haibun Online, Crannóg, Cyphers, Gorse, Haibun Today, The Incubator, The Irish Times, The Ofi Press, Poethead, Poetry Ireland Introductions: Selected Poems 2016, Poetry Ireland Review, Rise and Repeal Broadsheet, Skylight 47, Southword, The Stinging Fly, The Village*; and to the judges and organisers of the following competitions in which poems were either ranked or shortlisted: Allingham, Boyle, Dromineer, Francis Ledwidge, Free Wee Library, Gregory O'Donoghue, Redline and Strokestown.

'Immortality' is a found poem from *The Family Receipt Book*, 1837.

Thanks to Ray Kavanagh, whose book *Mamie Cadden: Backstreet Abortionist* (Mercier, 2015) I drew on for 'The Ballad of Mary Anne Cadden'.

The collection has been seven years in the making, and along the way has benefited greatly from the inspiration, support and friendship of the Hibernian Writers' Group, the staff and students of the Masters in Poetry Studies in Mater Dei (now DCU), and Jim Norton's haibun group.

Special thanks to Maurice Devitt, Sean O'Connor and Maeve O'Sullivan; Margaret Healion and Natasha Labe; Jane Clarke and Enda Wyley; to Niall Murphy for taking the cover photograph and to Patrick Redmond for the author photograph. Thanks to John Walsh and Lisa Frank of Doire Press for taking on the collection, and — as always — to my family.

AMANDA BELL is a professional member of the Irish Writers Centre and holds a Masters in Poetry Studies. Her haibun collection *Undercurrents* (Alba Publishing, 2016) was awarded second prize in the Haiku Society of America's Kanterman Merit Book Award and shortlisted for a Touchstone Distinguished Books Award by the Haiku Foundation. Her children's book *The Lost Library Book* was published by The Onslaught Press in May 2017. She was selected for Poetry Ireland's Introductions Series in 2016 and twice highly commended for the Patrick Kavanagh Award. In 2015 she won the William Allingham Poetry Prize and she is the editor of *Maurice Craig: Photographs* (Lilliput, 2011) and *The Lion Tamer Dreams of Office Work: An Anthology of Poetry by the Hibernian Writers* (Alba Publishing, 2015).

Visit her website at www.clearasabellwritingservices.ie.